It's Cinco de Mayo!

by Richard Sebra

BUMBA BOOKS™

LERNER PUBLICATIONS ◆ MINNEAPOLIS

Note to Educators:

Throughout this book, you'll find critical thinking questions. These can be used to engage young readers in thinking critically about the topic and in using the text and photos to do so.

Lerner Publications Company
A division of Lerner Publishing Group, Inc.
241 First Avenue North
Minneapolis, MN 55401 USA

For reading levels and more information, look up this title at www.lernerbooks.com.

Library of Congress Cataloging-in-Publication Data

Names: Sebra, Richard, 1984- author.
Title: It's Cinco de Mayo! / by Richard Sebra.
Description: Minneapolis : Lerner Publications, [2017] | Series: Bumba Books—It's a Holiday! | Includes bibliographical references and index.
Identifiers: LCCN 2016018671 (print) | LCCN 2016022497 (ebook) | ISBN 9781512425666 (lb : alk. paper) | ISBN 9781512429244 (pb : alk. paper) | ISBN 9781512427455 (eb pdf)
Subjects: LCSH: Cinco de Mayo (Mexican holiday)—Juvenile literature.
Classification: LCC F1233 .S43 2017 (print) | LCC F1233 (ebook) | DDC 394.262—dc23

LC record available at https://lccn.loc.gov/2016018671

Manufactured in the United States of America
1 – VP – 12/31/16

Expand learning beyond the printed book. Download free, complementary educational resources for this book from our website, www.lernerresource.com.

Table of Contents

Cinco de Mayo

Cinco de Mayo is a holiday.

It means "fifth of May" in Spanish.

Cinco de Mayo is May 5.

What does "cinco" mean in Spanish?

It is a Mexican holiday.

People in Mexico

celebrate.

People in the United

States celebrate too.

Cinco de Mayo honors a battle.

On May 5, 1862, Mexico won

a big battle.

Cinco de Mayo is a day to honor Mexican culture.

People eat Mexican food.

We eat tacos.

What are some other Mexican foods?

There are parades.

Many people watch

the parades.

Why do you think there are parades on holidays?

People dance too.

Dancers perform Mexican dances.

Many dancers dress

in Mexican clothing.

Women wear dresses.

The dresses are very colorful.

Cinco de Mayo is a day

to honor Mexico.

How do you celebrate

Cinco de Mayo?

Cinco de Mayo Symbols

Mexican flag

Mexican dress

sombrero

maracas

taco

Picture Glossary

bands

groups of musicians who perform together

battle

a fight between two armies

culture

the ideas, customs, and traditions of a group of people

honors

when a person or holiday praises or celebrates something

23

Index

Read More

Bullard, Lisa. *Marco's Cinco de Mayo.* Minneapolis: Millbrook Press, 2012.

Gleisner, Jenna Lee. *We Celebrate Cinco de Mayo in Spring.* Ann Arbor, MI: Cherry Lake Publishing, 2014.

Sebra, Richard. *It's Diwali!* Minneapolis: Lerner Publications, 2017.

Photo Credits

The images in this book are used with the permission of: © miker/Shutterstock.com, p. 5; © Tokarsky/iStock.com, pp. 6–7; © World History Archive/Alamy Stock Photo, pp. 9, 23 (top right); © Joshua Resnick/Dreamstime.com, pp. 10–11, 23 (bottom left); © Larry Wilmot/Dreamstime.com, pp. 12–13; © Doug Berry/iStock.com, pp. 14, 23 (top left); © valentinrussanov/iStock.com, p. 17; © Anna Bryukhanova/iStock.com, p. 18; © AbimelecOlan/iStock.com, pp. 21, 23 (bottom right); © stefano carniccio/Shutterstock.com, p. 22 (top left); © Leon Rafael/Shutterstock.com, p. 22 (top right); © Dja65/Shutterstock.com, p. 22 (middle); © Discovod/Shutterstock.com, p. 22 (bottom left); © ImagePixel/Shutterstock.com, p. 22 (bottom right).

Front Cover: © AbimelecOlan/iStock.com.